Patrick Chalmers

The Adhesive Postage Stamp

Patrick Chalmers

The Adhesive Postage Stamp

ISBN/EAN: 9783337864910

Printed in Europe, USA, Canada, Australia, Japan

Cover: Foto ©Thomas Meinert / pixelio.de

More available books at **www.hansebooks.com**

THE ADHESIVE POSTAGE STAMP.

DECISION OF THE
"ENCYCLOPÆDIA BRITANNICA":

James Chalmers was the Inventor of the Adhesive Stamp—" Mr. Pearson Hill has not weakened the Evidence" to that effect.

ALSO

𝕻apers on the 𝕻enny 𝕻ostage 𝕽eform,

BEQUEATHED BY THE LATE

SIR HENRY COLE.

JAMES CHALMERS FIRST PROPOSED THE ADOPTION OF THE ADHESIVE
POSTAGE STAMP,
OF WHICH HE WAS THE INVENTOR.

BY

PATRICK CHALMERS,

Fellow of the Royal Historical Society.

LONDON:
EFFINGHAM WILSON, ROYAL EXCHANGE.

1886.

Price Sixpence.

PREFACE.

WHEN a man of note dies, the journalist of the day can only reproduce in an obituary notice the accepted position of his life and works—it is no part of that writer's duty to examine, so as fully to certify, all the statements at hand, or to ransack old volumes dealing with the times when such reputation was established. That is the duty and the task of the later historian, or of some one specially interested. Such has been my duty, my task, as respects that public benefactor, the late Sir Rowland Hill, with the result arrived at in this and former publications.

Upon the death of Sir Rowland Hill in August, 1879, a series of letters with comments thereon appeared in the Dundee press, recalling the name and services of a townsman who, in his day, had taken an active interest in post-office improvement, and had worked in that field to some purpose. Mr. James Chalmers, bookseller, Dundee, who died in 1853, had been an earnest postal reformer. Through his efforts, and after a long correspondence with the Post Office in London, he brought about such an acceleration of the mail as to lessen the time necessary for the reply to a letter from Dundee to London, or betwixt the chief commercial towns of the north and south, by two days—a day each way. Subsequently he conceived the idea of an adhesive stamp for postage purposes ; and it was this invention, made known to such post-office reformers as Mr. Hume and Mr. Wallace—with both of whom, as with others, he was in communication—that formed the origin of the adoption of the adhesive stamp in the reformed Penny Postage system of 1840, the plan proposed by Mr. Rowland Hill in 1837 having been that of the impressed stamp.

These letters in the Dundee press from old townsmen and friends of Mr. Chalmers, personally unknown to me as I was to them (I having left Dundee while a youth, over fifty years ago, and passed much of the interval abroad), with the consequent attention drawn to the subject, naturally called upon me to make an endeavour to vindicate my father's claim to the merit of such an important feature in the success of the Penny Postage scheme as was, and is, the adhesive stamp. These letters, moreover, acquainted me with what I was previously unaware of—that on the 1st January, 1846, a public testimonial had been presented in the Town Hall of Dundee to Mr. Chalmers, in recognition of his postal services, and of his having been the originator of the adhesive postage stamp; thus all the more calling upon me to investigate a subject of which hitherto I had only a dim and partial idea. This investigation was further facilitated by my withdrawal just before the same period of 1879 from active business, thus enabling me to examine at the library of the British Museum the papers, documents, speeches, and motions in Parliament, Reports of Parliamentary Committees, and all such evidence and information tending to throw light upon, from the year 1832 onwards, the history and events preceding the reformed system of postage introduced to the public in the year 1837 by the then Mr. Rowland Hill.

My father long since dead (while I was abroad), and his establishment long ago broken up, difficulty was at first experienced in obtaining the specific evidence necessary to enable me to establish my claim on his behalf, but the attention publicly drawn to the matter by former publications of my own, and of Mr. Pearson Hill to which I was called upon to reply, brought forward ever-increasing evidence of the most conclusive nature, and to which I am now enabled to add material and interesting confirmation from papers left by the late Sir Henry Cole, whose connection with the Penny Postage Reform of 1837–40 is well known.

THE

PENNY POSTAGE SCHEME OF SIR ROWLAND HILL NOT ORIGINAL.

My business, of course, in the investigation just named, was to ascertain what plan Sir Rowland Hill had proposed in his pamphlet of 1837 for the purpose of carrying out his Penny Postage Scheme, and to trace therefrom the adoption on his part of my father's plan of the adhesive stamp. But a discovery of much more historical importance before long presented itself, namely, that neither the conception of uniform penny postage itself, nor of any one of the valuable principles and figures of the penny postage scheme, were original conceptions on the part of Sir Rowland Hill.

The reformed system of postage was not the work of one year nor of one man. For some years prior to 1837 the abuses and mismanagement of the post office were a constant theme of complaint, both in and out of Parliament—many able and earnest men combined to bring about some reform demanded by men of business and public opinion. Commissions of inquiry were held, evidence and suggestions taken, reports issued. Early in 1835 Mr. Wallace, M.P. for Greenock, a prominent post-office reformer, obtained a Commission of Inquiry on the subject, which Commission issued in all ten Reports; while, in addition to Parliamentary returns, a commission, termed the Commission of Revenue Inquiry, had sat for many years prior to the Commission of merely Post Office Inquiry, and had issued twenty-three Reports, in more than one of which post-office affairs were dealt with.

In that large field of complaint, suggestion, information, and proposal may be found the substance, origin, and foundation of the subsequent writings and proposals of Sir Rowland Hill.

It will be remembered that the old system of postage, prior to 1840, was that of a high and variable charge according to distance, of, say, twopence to one shilling and sixpence a letter, charged by sheet; and two sheets, however light in weight, were charged double. The same with circulars. But in these Reports, including the evidence of the numerous witnesses, are to be found embodied all the valuable principles and figures of the reformed system. And that all these Reports had come under Mr. Hill's review is left in no doubt, having been sent to him by Mr. Wallace, after Mr. Hill, freed from other occupations, had, in 1835, joined the circle of post-office reformers, when he " commenced that

" systematic study, analysis, and comparison
" which the difficulty of my self-imposed task
" rendered necessary."—(" Life," page 246.)

But to be looked upon as the *inventor* of that
scheme which he had introduced and (saved and
rendered practicable by the adhesive stamp) had
successfully carried out—to have this scheme
understood as having been the unaided conception
of his own mind—was with Sir Rowland Hill
simply a mania, and to that mania James
Chalmers, the originator in every sense of that
adhesive stamp, was sacrificed.

The bearing of all this non-originality of conception on the part of Sir Rowland Hill is obvious
when the question of the stamp is under consideration. In propounding the scheme itself,
what were only acquired ideas were assumed, or
allowed to be assumed, as inventions or conceptions. As with the scheme, so with the stamp—
the stamp also was an acquired idea, not Rowland
Hill's invention.

Having now, however, obtained from a quarter
of the highest standing, after an impartial investigation, a full acknowledgment of my father's
services, and this in addition to an already large
amount of recognition from the press in general,
further observations as to the non-originality of
the scheme may be here dispensed with, for the
present at least, and left to history. And if I
have been compelled to show that, so far from the

adhesive stamp having been the invention of Sir
Rowland Hill, originality of conception formed no
element whatever in any one of the proposals of
even the Penny Postage Scheme itself, such
course has been forced upon me by the unfortunate proceedings of Mr. Pearson Hill in denying,
against the clearest evidence, my just claim in
the matter of the stamp, without a pretence of
proof that such was at any period an invention
on the part of Sir Rowland Hill.

THE IMPRESSED STAMP.

THE plan by which Mr. Rowland Hill, in his pamphlet of 1837, proposed to carry out in practice his uniform penny postage scheme was, shortly stated, first, simply to pay the penny or money with the letters; but secondly, and more especially, by stamped sheets of letter paper, and stamped wrappers or covers. "Let stamped covers and "sheets of paper be supplied to the public, from "the Stamp Office or Post Office, or both, and at "such a price as to include the postage." . . . "Economy and the public convenience would "require that sheets of letter paper of every "description should be stamped on the part used "for the address; that wrappers, such as are "used for newspapers, as well as covers made of "cheap paper, should also be stamped," and kept on sale at the post offices. "Stationers would also "be induced to keep them."

What Mr. Hill overlooked in this proposal, was the broad fact that he sets up the Stamp Office or Post Office to do the business in letter paper of the stationers throughout the kingdom—some huge Government establishment against which competition would be hopeless, as the Stamp Office was to sell the writing paper at cost price, while the stationer requires a profit to pay his rent and expenses, and to live upon. The effect upon the stationers, consequently would have been confiscation—and against this plan the united body of paper makers and stationers subsequently protested.

The Select Committee of the House of Commons of 1837-38, again, took exception to Mr. Hill's plan mainly on account of its liability to forgery— a stamp of the nature proposed would be extensively forged. After evidence on the part of the Stamp-Office authorities and paper makers had been taken, it was decided to recommend—that the paper for all stamped covers should be manufactured at the paper mills of a Mr. Dickenson, or of another, solely, under strict excise supervision. This paper of Mr. Dickenson's was of a peculiar make, having threads of cotton or silk so interwoven in the paper that a post-office clerk could readily know by the look or feel that a stamped cover was genuine. The paper makers protested and petitioned against this, objecting to one of the body having all the work. Besides, the proposal involved permanent excise supervision over the manufacture of paper. This proposal, however, extended only to covers or envelopes; how forgery was to be prevented in respect to the stamps upon the sheets of letter paper the Committee do not say. The whole position, in fact, remained in a state of chaos, only relieved by the ultimate adoption of the adhesive stamp, which plan Mr. Chalmers had laid before this Committee through Mr. Wallace, the Chairman, and likewise through Mr. Chalmers, M.P., a member of the Committee, and which plan had been publicly discussed, not without finding adherents, including Mr. Cobden, one of the witnesses in favour of the scheme.

To the solution proposed by the Committee that all stamped covers should be made of Dickenson's peculiar paper the Government again highly objected, further adding to the dilemma; and when the Chancellor of the Exchequer, on the 5th of July, 1839, introduced and carried a resolution sanctioning a Penny Postage Bill being brought forward, he distinctly only " asked hon. " members to commit themselves to the question " of a uniform rate of postage of one penny at and " under a weight hereafter to be fixed." Everything else was to be left open. " If it were to " go forth to the public to-morrow morning that " the Government had proposed, and the House " had adopted, the plan of Mr. Rowland Hill, the " necessary result would be to spread a conviction " abroad that, as a stamped cover was absolutely " to be used in all cases, which stamped covers " were to be made by one single manufacturer, " alarm would be felt lest a monopoly would " thereby be created, to the serious detriment of

" other members of a most useful and important
" trade. The sense of injustice excited by this
" would necessarily be extreme. I therefore do
" not call upon the House either to affirm or to
" negative any such proposition at the present.
" I ask you simply to affirm the adoption of a
" uniform penny postage, and the taxation of that
" postage by weight. Neither do I ask you to
" pledge yourselves to the prepayment of letters,
" for I am of opinion that, at all events, there
" should be an option of putting letters into the
" post without a stamp."

" If the resolution be affirmed, and the Bill has
" to be proposed, it will hereafter require very
" great care and complicated arrangements to
" carry the plan into practical effect. It may
" involve considerable expense and considerable
" responsibility on the part of the Government;
" it may disturb existing trades, such as the paper
" trade." . . . "The new postage will be
" distinctly and simply a penny postage by weight."

. . " I also require for the Treasury a power
" of taking the postage by anticipation, and a
" power of allowing such postage to be taken by
" means of stamped covers, and I also require the
" authority of rating the postage according to
" weight." *

In this dilemma, as to *how* to carry out the
scheme in practice, Mr. Wallace favourably sug-

---

* See " Hansard," Vol. 48.

gested the adhesive stamp, the adoption of which plan, he had no hesitation in saying from the evidence adduced, would secure the revenue from loss by forgery. Mr. Warburton, also a member of the 1837-38 Committee, " viewing with consider-" able alarm the doubt which had been expressed " of adopting Mr. Hill's plan of prepayment and " collection by stamped covers," recommended that plans should be applied for from the public.

Again, in the House of Lords on the 5th of August, Lord Melbourne, in introducing the Bill, is as much embarrassed as was the Chancellor of the Exchequer in the Commons. The opponents of the Bill use, as one of their strongest arguments, the impossibility of carrying out the scheme in practice. The Earl of Ripon says :— " Why were their lordships thus called upon at " this period of the session to pass a Bill, when " no mortal being at that moment had the re-" motest conception of how it was to be carried " into execution ? " Here Lord Ashburton, like Mr. Wallace in the Commons, favourably suggested the adhesive stamp, " which would answer " every purpose, and remove the objection of the " stationers and paper makers to the measure."

Let it, then, be clearly noted that, up to the period of the Bill in July and August, 1839, not a word is said in any way connecting Mr. Hill's name with other than the impressed stamp on the sheet of letter paper, or, more especially, on the

stamped covers. That, *and that alone*, is taken on
the one part as *his* plan by all the speakers,
official or otherwise — for that alone does the
Chancellor of the Exchequer ask for "powers."
The adhesive stamp is brought in, on the other
part, as a distinct proposal, in no way entering
into the proposals of Mr. Hill.

(The above is given in more detail in my
former pamphlet, entitled "Sir Rowland Hill
and James Chalmers, the Inventor of the Adhesive Stamp," 1883).

THE ADHESIVE STAMP.

In my pamphlet entitled "Sir Rowland Hill and "James Chalmers, the Inventor of the Adhesive "Stamp," I have already proved from overwhelming evidence, both general and specific, the invention of the adhesive stamp for postage purposes by the late James Chalmers, bookseller, Dundee, in the month of August, 1834. In addition to friends and fellow-townsmen, several of those in his employment at that period have, unknown to me, come forward from various quarters to describe the process and to fix the date. The setting up of the form with a number of stamps having a printed device—the printing of the sheets—the melting of the gum—the gumming the backs of the sheets—the drying and the pressing—are all described, and the date already named is conclusively fixed.* That this was the first instance of such invention is clear; earlier instances of an

---

* Since publishing my evidence specifically proving what is here stated, I have been favoured with the following letter :—

" BRECHIN,
9th October, 1883

" DEAR SIR,

" When I penned my anonymous note to the *Dundee Advertiser* " in August, 1879, expressing the hope that there might be still living " some who could corroborate my statement that the late Mr. Chalmers " was the inventor of the 'Adhesive Stamp,' I hardly expected it would " be followed by such an amount of corroboration.

" With regard to the *date* of the invention, you appear to have received " ample proof, and I am able to add thereto. It was in the autumn of

B

impressed stamp proposed for postage purposes are on record, but not one of a proposed adhesive stamp—while Sir Rowland Hill himself has left it on record, in his " Life," referring to the same period and occasion when an impressed stamp was proposed in 1834 for newspaper covers by Mr. Knight, " of course, adhesive stamps were " yet undreamt of." (See page 69 of my pamphlet above named).

I have further shown that Mr. Chalmers was one of the early postal reformers prior to the period of Mr. Rowland Hill, that he had done great service in the way of accelerating the mails betwixt London and the north, and that he was in communication with several of those early reformers, such as Mr. Hume, Mr. Wallace, and Mr. Knight—the publisher subsequently of Mr.

" 1834 that I left Dundee to reside here, and the Stamp was in existence " in Mr. Chalmers' premises before I left.

" I may add that when I wrote in 1879, I was not aware of the " existence of a son of Mr. C. My sole object in writing was that *Dundee* " might claim and receive the honour of being the place of birth of the " ' Adhesive Stamp.'

" I am, &c.,

" P. CHALMERS, Esq.,   " (*Signed*)   DAVID PRAIN.
     " Wimbledon."

A Portrait of Mr. Prain, by the talented Scottish artist, Mr. Irvine, subscribed for by Mr. Prain's fellow-townsmen and former pupils, has just been presented in his honour to the Mechanic's Institute of Brechin. The proceedings upon this occasion, including the able speeches of Provost Lamb and of Mr. Prain, will be found in the *Brechin Advertiser* of 16th June, 1885. On a former occasion Mr. Prain was presented with a Service of Plate and Testimonial to the value of several hundred pounds, subscribed for by former pupils at home and abroad. It is at the testimony of such men as this, including the late Mr. William Thoms, of Dundee, that my opponents sneer as being " the mere wandering fancies of a few old men ! " The general testimony is that of an entire locality.

Rowland Hill's pamphlet of 1837—so that his proposal of an adhesive stamp for postage purposes, a matter of notoriety in his own locality, would further have become well known in the general circle of postal reformers, amongst whom, and from whom, on joining same in the year 1835, Mr. Rowland Hill obtained the information which enabled him to draw up and publish his Penny Postage Scheme of 1837. (See page 5 of my pamphlet named.)

One of those pioneers of postal reform, the Rev. Samuel Roberts, M.A., of Conway, gives his personal testimony of the adhesive stamp having been originated by James Chalmers. (Page 42.)*

My pamphlet goes on to show (page 44) that on the appointment of the House of Commons Committee of 1837-38 on the proposed uniform Penny Postage Scheme, Mr. Chalmers sent in his plan of an adhesive stamp to Mr. Wallace, the Chairman, and to another Member of that Committee. Mr. Wallace's reply, stating that he will lay the plan before the Committee, is of date 9th December, 1837. In the dilemma in which the Government found itself (upon introducing on the 5th July, 1839, the Resolution preliminary to the Bill) as to *how* to carry out the Penny Postage Scheme in practice (page 21) Mr. Wallace favour-

---

* An interesting obituary of Mr. Roberts, lately deceased, will be found in the "*Times*" of 30th September, 1885. Mr. Roberts is there recognised as the pioneer of postal reform and originator of the proposal of a low and uniform postage.

ably suggested the plan of the adhesive stamp. The statement of the Chancellor of the Exchequer upon this occasion, with the interposition of Mr. Wallace in the Commons, and of Lord Ashburton in the Lords, in favour of the adhesive stamp have already been given, conclusively showing that, up to this period, Mr. Hill had not included the adhesive stamp in his proposals.

On the passing of the Bill in August, Mr. Hill was relegated to the Treasury for the purpose of carrying out the scheme. The first step taken was to invite plans, by Treasury Circular of 23rd August, from the public; some time was taken up in receiving and considering these plans, until, by Treasury Minute of December 26th, 1839, the adhesive stamp was at length officially adopted, in conjunction with Mr. Hill's stamped covers, or stamp impressed upon the sheet of letter paper itself. (See page 46.) But the adhesive stamp, indeed, had been practically adopted by Mr. Hill before the plans were received, considered, and nothing better found, a concurrence of opinion having set in in favour of same. It will be seen that Mr. Chalmers, in his published statement of date February, 1838, now produced from Sir Henry Cole's papers, called for petitions towards the adoption of the adhesive stamp. In August, 1839, both the Associated Body of Paper-Makers and certain Merchants and Bankers of the City of London pressed for the adoption of this stamp; Mr. Rowland Hill himself, in a paper entitled " On the Collection of Postage by means of Stamps," circulated by him about the period of the Bill being before Parliament, included the adoption of the adhesive stamp, in conjunction with his own impressed stamp. Mr. Cole also drew up an able paper on the stamp question, including the advocacy of the adhesive stamp. So general, indeed, had then become opinion in its favour, that of the plans sent in no less than forty-nine others besides Mr. Chalmers, who again sent in his plan, recommended the adoption of the adhesive stamp, invented by Mr. Chalmers in 1834, laid by him before the Committee of the House of Commons in December, 1837, and further, as we shall now see, sent in to Mr. Cole as Secretary to the Mercantile Committee of the City of London, in February, 1838, and acknowledged by Mr. Rowland Hill· in a letter to Mr. Chalmers of date 3rd March, 1838. In this letter Mr. Hill makes no pretension to the merit or proposed adoption of the adhesive stamp on his part, for, as will be seen, Mr. Chalmers subsequently returned to Mr. Hill a copy of this very letter for the purpose of pointing out this fact to Mr. Hill. It was not until the propriety, and indeed necessity, of adopting Mr. Chalmers' plan —not until its final official acceptance—that, in a letter dated 18th January, 1840, Mr. Hill, then in despotic power, putting Mr. Chalmers aside upon the pretext afterwards mentioned, assumed the whole merit to himself.

SIR HENRY COLE'S PAPERS

AND THE

ADHESIVE STAMP OF MR. CHALMERS.

In his " Fifty Years of Public Life," lately published, Sir Henry Cole gives much information
with respect to the Penny Postage reform, a boon
with the obtaining and carrying out of which he
was intimately associated—first as secretary to the
Mercantile Committee of the City of London, and
afterwards as coadjutor to Mr. Rowland Hill at the
Treasury. "A General Collection of Postage
" Papers," having reference to this reform, elucidating the efforts made by this Committee of
London Merchants and Bankers during the year
1838–39, to obtain for the scheme the sanction of
the Legislature, has been bequeathed by Sir Henry
Cole, " to be given to the British Museum after
" my death."* " The Mercantile Committee," he
states, " was formed chiefly by the exertions of
" Mr. George Moffat in the spring of 1838.
" Mr. Ashurst conducted the Parliamentary In-

---

* These papers are in the Art Library of the South Kensington Museum.

" quiry, and upon myself, as Secretary, devolved
" the business of communicating with the public."
This Committee formed the source and focus of
the agitation which brought about the ultimate
enactment of uniform Penny Postage. Money
was freely subscribed, meetings were held, public
bodies in the provinces were urged to petition,
Members of Parliament and Ministers were waited
upon, and a special paper advocating the scheme,
termed the "Post Circular," was issued and
circulated gratis. Of these proceedings Mr. Cole
was the guiding genius; and, amongst other
successes, over two thousand petitions to Parliament were obtained—labours which were ultimately
crowned with success.

To Mr. Cole, then, it now turns out that
Mr. Chalmers, in February, 1838, sent a copy of
his plan of the adhesive stamp. Mr. Wallace and
the House of Commons Committee had already
got it, but it is only now that the particulars of the
plan have been brought to light—and in this
"Collection of Postage Papers," Sir Henry Cole
has indeed left a valuable legacy to me, and to
all prepared to recognise the true originator of the
adhesive postage stamp. These papers include
a printed statement of Mr. Chalmers' plan, dated
"4 Castle Street, Dundee, 8th February, 1838,"
and which runs as follows :—

" *Remarks on various modes proposed for franking*
   " *letters, under Mr. Rowland Hill's Plan of Post*
   " *Office Reform.*

" In suggesting any method of improvement, it
" is only reasonable to expect that what are sup-
" posed to be its advantages over any existing
" system, or in opposition to others that have been
" or may be proposed, will be explicitly stated.

" Therefore, if Mr. Hill's plan of a uniform rate
" of postage, and that all postages are to be paid
" by those sending letters *before* they are deposited
" in the respective post offices, become the law of
" the land, I conceive that the most simple and
" economical mode of carrying out such an ar-
" rangement would be by *slips* (postage stamps)
" prepared somewhat similar to the specimens
" herewith shown.

" With this view, and in the hope that Mr.
" Hill's plan may soon be carried into operation,
" I would suggest that sheets of stamped slips
" should be prepared at the Stamp Office (on a
" paper made expressly for the purpose) with a
" device on each for a die or cut resembling that
" on newspapers ; that the *sheets* so printed or
" stamped should then be rubbed over with a
" strong solution of gum or other adhesive sub-
" stance, and (when thoroughly dry) issued by
" the Stamp Office to town and country dis-
" tributors, to stationers and others, for sale in
" sheets or singly, under the same laws and re-

" strictions now applicable to those selling bill or
" receipt stamps, so as to prevent, as far as prac-
" ticable, any fraud on the revenue.

" Merchants and others whose correspondence
" is extensive, could purchase these slips in quan-
" tities, cut them singly, and affix one to a letter
" by means of wetting the back of the slip with a
" sponge or brush, just with as much facility as
" applying a wafer."—Adding that in some cases,
such as for circulars, the stamp might answer
both for stamp and wafer; a suggestion which
those who may recollect the mode of folding
universally practised before the days of envelopes,
will appreciate. Mr. Chalmers goes on—" Others,
" requiring only one or two slips at a time, could
" purchase them along with sheets of paper at
" stationers' shops, the *weight* only regulating the
" rate of postage in all cases, so as a stamp may
" be affixed according so the scale determined on.

" Again, to prevent the possibility of these
" being used a *second time*, it should be made
" imperative on postmasters to put the post office
" town stamp (as represented in one of the speci-
" mens), across the slip or postage stamp."

Mr. Chalmers then goes on to point out the
advantages to be derived from this plan, and to
state objections to Mr. Hill's plan of impressed
stamped covers or envelopes, or stamp impressed
upon the sheet of letter paper itself. At that
period envelopes — being scarcely known, and

never used, as involving double postage—were a hand-made article, heavy and expensive; objections which have disappeared with the abolition of the Excise duty on paper, and the use of machinery. But how true were Mr. Chalmers' objections *then*, may be gathered from the fact, as recorded by Sir Rowland Hill in his "Life," that the large supply provided of the first postage envelope, the Mulready, had actually *to be destroyed* as wholly unsuitable and unsaleable, while the supply of adhesive stamps was with difficulty brought up to the demand. The force and value of Mr. Chalmers' objections to the stamp impressed upon the sheet itself, are best exemplified by the fact that, though ultimately sanctioned by the Treasury at the instance of Mr. Hill, such plan never came into use. People bought their own paper from the stationers, and not from the Stamp Office, and applied the adhesive stamp as the weight required. Mr. Chalmers concludes, " taking all these disadvantages into considera- " tion, the use of stamped slips is certainly the " most preferable system; and, should others " who take an interest in the proposed reform " view the matter in the same light as I do, it " remains for them to petition Parliament to have " such carried into operation."

This statement of Mr. Chalmers is printed on part of an elongated sheet of paper. On the half not occupied by the type are several specimens of a suggested stamp, about an inch square, and with the words printed, "General Postage—not ex-" ceeding half-an-ounce—One Penny." And the same—"Not exceeding one ounce—Twopence." (It is only of late years that a penny has franked one ounce in weight.) A space divides each stamp for cutting off singly,* and the back of the sheet is gummed over. One of the specimens is stamped across with the post-mark, "Dundee, "10th February, 1838," to exemplify what Mr. Chalmers states should be done to prevent the stamp being used a second time.

Here is a complete description of the principle of the adhesive stamp as ultimately adopted by Mr. Hill at the Treasury by Minute of 26th December, 1839, when he sent Mr. Cole to Messrs. Bacon & Petch, the eminent engravers, to provide a die and contract for the supply of stamps (see Mr. Bacon's evidence, page 52 of my former Pamphlet), a plan in use to the present day.

This description, as now brought to light under the signature of Mr. Chalmers himself, fully confirms the evidence with respect to the invention in August, 1834, as given by his then *employés* yet living, W. Whitelaw and others. (See pages 34–39 of my former pamphlet.)

Here, then, was the plan of the future adhesive

---

* The perforated sheets were not introduced until the year 1852. This improvement was the invention of a Mr. Archer, for which he got the sum of £4,000.

stamp, already laid before Mr. Wallace and the
House of Commons Committee, also sent to the
Secretary of the City of London Mercantile Committee, in printed form, as to one of many, long
before leave was asked, on 5th July, 1839, even
to introduce the Bill into Parliament. That
Mr. Hill saw Mr. Cole's copy, or had a special
copy sent also to himself, is clear, because
Mr. Hill at once writes to Mr. Chalmers, under
date 3rd March, 1838. What Mr. Hill states in
that letter we know not altogether, as Mr. Pearson
Hill has not thought proper to publish that letter,
and my request to him for a copy has not been
complied with. (See page 64 of my former
pamphlet.) We know thus much, however, that
Mr. Rowland Hill makes no pretension *then* to
ever having suggested or approved of an adhesive
stamp, as already pointed out. Not until writing
to Mr. Chalmers on the 18th January, 1840 (see
page 62 of former pamphlet), before which
period, in obedience to the general demand, the
adhesive stamp had at length been adopted, did
Mr. Hill, in reply to Mr. Chalmers' claim as the
originator, set up any counter-claim on his own
part to any share in the merit of the adhesive
stamp. But, as with the scheme itself, so now
with the stamp which saved it, no second party
was to be allowed to divide with Mr. Hill the sole
merit of this great reform. So the far-fetched
excuse, the mere afterthought, bred of the

success which had attended Mr. Chalmers' proposal to the Committee and to Mr. Cole, is hit upon (page 54) to put Mr. Chalmers aside and to attach to himself the whole merit of the adhesive stamp./ Mr. Hill had said something about a bit of gummed paper before the Commissioners of Post Office Inquiry in February, 1837 (subsequent to publishing the first edition of his pamphlet, in which nothing was said of an adhesive stamp), an idea Mr. Hill had acquired in the interval, just as he had acquired all the principles of the scheme itself, at second hand. (page 60). On this occasion Mr. Hill had supposed a difficulty which might occur to a person who had to re-address a letter at a Post Office, but was unable to write, and at the same time precluded from paying the penny in cash, while the stamped wrapper would obliterate the address. In such an exceptional case, and in order to secure "the universal adoption" of the impressed stamp, a bit of paper just large enough to bear the stamp, and covered at the back with a glutinous wash, might be wetted and applied. Better, however, he goes on to say, allow the penny to be received in cash, so that you have only the impressed stamp or the penny in payment, and which penny was accepted up to the year 1855.* Up to the

---

* In his "Life" lately published, written by himself, Sir Rowland Hill *omits the clause* in his original evidence which restores the payment of the penny in cash and does away with any necessity for an adhesive stamp, even in the exceptional case he had supposed. Not only does Sir Rowland

year 1855, consequently, no such exceptional case could have arisen, the penny in cash being sufficient acceptance. This allusion to an adhesive stamp is repeated by Mr. Hill in the second edition of his pamphlet. Here then, in February, 1837, was a passing allusion made by Mr. Hill to an adhesive stamp, showing that, subsequent to the issue of the first edition of his pamphlet, he had acquired from some quarter the idea of Mr. Chalmers' invention. February, 1837, was two years and a half after the proved invention of the adhesive stamp by Mr. Chalmers, one of the early postal reformers, one who "held correspond-" ence with the postal reformers of his day, both " in and out of Parliament " (" Encyclopædia Britannica," see page 39 following), the correspondent, amongst others, of Messrs. Knight & Co., who published for Mr. Hill. In a letter, then, of 18th January, 1840, as we learn from Mr. Pearson Hill's account of the matter, and from Mr. Chalmers' reply, Mr. Hill pointed out to Mr. Chalmers that his claim could not be admitted, because he, Mr. Hill, first proposed an adhesive stamp in February, 1837, the first official proposal of his plan by Mr. Chalmers, his letter to Mr. Wallace

---

Hill omit this clause, but he even gives the reader to understand that to the year 1837, the year of his pamphlet, is to be ascribed his adoption of the adhesive stamp. How then, it will be asked, does Sir Rowland Hill account for the speech of the Chancellor of the Exchequer on the 5th July, 1839, and the interposition of Mr. Wallace in favour of an adhesive stamp? This difficulty Sir Rowland Hill surmounts by simply taking no notice of either.

and the House of Commons Committee, having been only in December of the same year. In answer to this extraordinary pretension on the part of Mr. Hill, it is enough to point to Mr. Hill's letters to the Postmaster-General, Lord Litchfield, in January, 1838, explaining and enforcing his penny postage scheme then before the public— letters published in the papers of the period, and in which not a word is said of an adhesive stamp.* Or more than enough, to point to the speech of the Chancellor of the Exchequer, already quoted (page 13), to prove that, up to so late a date as the 5th July, 1839, Mr. Hill had *not* proposed to adopt an adhesive stamp. The press, up to 30th August, 1839, had heard of no such proposal on his part.†

This allusion to an adhesive stamp in February, 1837, was a mere passing allusion as to what

---

* In his letter to Lord Litchfield of 9th January, 1838, Mr. Hill states his plan to be :—"That the payment should always be in advance. And " to rid this mode of payment of the trouble and risk which it would " otherwise entail on the sending of letters, as well as for other important " considerations, I propose that the postage be collected by the sale of " stamped covers."

† The "Times" of this date has the following paragraph :—"The Penny " Postage will commence, we learn, on the 1st January next. It is " intended that stamped envelopes shall be sold at every Post Office, so " that stationers and other shopkeepers may, as well as the public, supply " themselves at a minute's notice." Not a word as to an Adhesive Stamp being known as in contemplation. It will be evident from these two instances alone, independent of the proceedings in Parliament and of Mr. Hill's letter to Mr. Chalmers of 3rd March, 1838, that the Adhesive Stamp formed no part of the original proposals or intentions of Sir Rowland Hill.

might be done in a supposed exceptional case which could never have arisen so long as the penny in cash was accepted, and was nothing more. For Mr. Hill to represent to Mr. Chalmers that he, Mr. Hill, had proposed to adopt the adhesive stamp as a means of carrying out his scheme in February, 1837, was to state what was *not the case;* consequently any admission so gained from Mr. Chalmers was wholly invalid. An extract from the reply of Mr. Chalmers, dated 18th May, 1840 (reproduced at page 62 of my former pamphlet), has been circulated by Mr. Pearson Hill, in whose hands alone is the entire correspondence, with the object of showing that Mr. Chalmers " honestly abandoned " his claim. But Mr. Chalmers honestly abandoned nothing; while no impartial person will, upon considera- tion, for a moment attach any importance to just what " extract " from his correspondence Mr. Pearson Hill has thought proper to produce. I again contend, as I have already maintained, that this correspondence was public, not private, pro- perty — that such should have remained at the Treasury, subject to the inspection of all con- cerned, in place of having been appropriated by Sir Rowland Hill as private, and thus so as to admit of only such portion being ultimately made known as may have suited himself. In this extract of 18th May, 1840, Mr. Chalmers, after stating he had delayed to reply until seeing the stamps in operation, writes with surprise at what Mr. Hill now states. Had he known or supposed that any one else, especially Mr. Hill himself, had proposed the adhesive stamp for the purpose of carrying out the scheme, he would not have troubled him at all. But having sent his plan to Mr. Wallace, M.P., and got his acknowledgment of 9th December, 1837, saying same would be laid before the Committee; also to Mr. Chalmers, M.P., and got his reply of 7th October, 1839, saying such had been laid before the Committee; also Mr. Hill's own letter of 3rd March, 1838, a copy of which he encloses—from *all* these he was led to believe he had been first in the field. *Now*, not doubting Mr. Hill's assurance of 18th January, 1840, to the contrary (and in any case indisposed to contest a decision against which there was practically no appeal), he only regrets having through his ignorance put others as well as himself to any trouble in the matter; "while the " only satisfaction I have had in this as well as in " former suggestions—all original with me—is " that these have been adopted, and have been " and are likely to prove beneficial to the public."

Such is the letter or extract which, placed in the hands of every editor in London, has led to my statements being here treated with compara- tive neglect.* But let my statements equally

---

* See "The World," "Daily Chronicle," &c., also "Proceedings of the Commissioners of Sewers" for July, 1881, as reported in the "City Press."

with those of Mr. Pearson Hill be read by any
impartial writer, as in the case of the "Encyclo-
"pædia Britannica," afterwards noticed, and the
result, it will be seen, is to lead to an entirely
different conclusion. "James Chalmers was the
"inventor of the adhesive postage stamp —
"Mr. Pearson Hill has not weakened the evidence
"to that effect." Here was honesty certainly—
simplicity indeed—on the side of Mr. Chalmers;
but what about the representation on the part of
Mr. Hill? Was it the case that he had proposed
the adoption of the adhesive stamp in February,
1837, as represented to Mr. Chalmers? The
proofs to the contrary are conclusive. Mr. Hill
had made a passing allusion to an adhesive stamp
in February, 1837, but *only* a passing allusion.
Nothing can be more clear than that the adoption of the adhesive stamp for the purpose of
carrying out his scheme formed no part of the
original proposals and intentions of Mr. Hill.
His representation to Mr. Chalmers was therefore exaggerated, delusive, and misleading.*
"Why did not you tell me anything of this
"before?' replies Mr. Chalmers in effect;—
"*there* is a copy of your letter of 3rd March,
"1838, when I sent you my plan, in which letter

---

* The "Christian Leader" of Glasgow ably puts the matter thus :—
"Sir Rowland Hill seems to have been at pains to obscure the facts of the
"case for the purpose of claiming to himself the credit of an invention
"which really belonged to the Dundee bookseller."

" of yours no such pretensions were put forward.
" It is only now that I learn for the first time that
" you had ever proposed or been in favour of an
" adhesive stamp. Further, how is it that neither
" of these members of the Committee before whom
" I laid my plan had ever heard of any such prior
" proposal on your part? However, I am now
" only sorry at having troubled you—I have at
" least the satisfaction of knowing that the public
" have got my plan somehow."

" Why did you not tell me anything of this
" before?" Why indeed! Because Mr. Hill *then* had
not contemplated an adhesive stamp, as has been
abundantly proved. An impressed stamped cover
" was absolutely to be used in all cases," says the.
Chancellor of the Exchequer as late as in July,
1839—a " power" was asked for this, and for
this alone. (See *ante*, page 14.) But much had
happened in the interval betwixt Mr. Hill's two
letters to Mr. Chalmers. The stamp not accepted
by Mr. Hill in 1838 had become in 1840 the
favourite of all opinions concerned, the adopted
of the Treasury. It had saved his scheme.
Mr. Chalmers must now be put aside, a matter
which the entire contrast betwixt the dispositions
of the two men rendered only too easy, and so
this afterthought, this far-fetched pretext already
noticed, was hit upon for the purpose.

At the same time Mr. Chalmers appears to
have been too apathetic in the matter, indifferent

to personal considerations so long as the public got his stamp from some quarter ; but the absence of any desire for personal advantage is a not unfrequent characteristic in those who have done some public service.

But it is this neglect, or mere indifference, on the part of my father, in not having made a better stand in 1840 with respect to a matter the national and universal value of which no one could then appreciate or foresee, that all the more calls upon me now, under a better acquaintance with the facts and circumstances, to claim for his memory that recognition to which he is clearly entitled, as having been " The Originator and Inventor of the " Adhesive Postage Stamp."

THE "ENCYCLOPÆDIA BRITANNICA."

THE nineteenth volume of the above-named standard work, lately published, contains an article headed "Postage Stamps," in which my late father is fully recognised as having been the inventor of the adhesive postage stamp. It is well known that the articles in this work are drawn up by learned experts upon the respective subjects dealt with, having access to and being in the habit of consulting official and historical documents, and edited under a strong sense of responsibility to the high standing of the work itself and to history; so that it is with unspeakable satisfaction that I now find myself enabled to produce from such a quarter an emphatic recognition of my father's services in connection with the great boon of Penny Postage reform.

This article, so far as it deals with the origin of the adhesive stamp, is as follows; but in considering same it should be borne in mind that the article was drawn up *before* the discovery of Mr. Chalmers' plan amongst the papers of the late Sir Henry Cole, with the consequent proofs given in the last chapter as to Mr. Chalmers having taken the initiative in urging the adoption of this stamp, not only to Members of the Select Com-

mittee of the House of Commons of 1837–38, but
to Mr. Rowland Hill himself, long before Mr. Hill,
in his paper of 1839 (see *ante*, page 21), gave in
his adhesion to that plan in conjunction with
his own :—

  "POSTAGE STAMPS.—For all practical pur-
" poses the history of postage stamps begins in
" the United Kingdom, and with the great reform
" of its postal system in 1839–40." After giving
instances in which the *impressed* stamp had been
in use, or had been suggested for postal purposes in this country and elsewhere, the article
proceeds :—" Finally, and in its results most im-
" portant of all, the ' adhesive stamp' was made,
" experimentally, in his printing-office at Dundee,
" by Mr. James Chalmers, in August, 1834.*
" These experimental stamps were printed from
" ordinary type, and were made adhesive by a
" wash of gum.   Their inventor had already

---

* "Patrick Chalmers, Sir Rowland Hill, and James Chalmers, Inventor
" of the Adhesive Stamp (London, 1882), *passim*." See also the same
writer's pamphlet, entitled "The Position of Sir Rowland Hill made plain
(1882)," and his "The Adhesive Stamp ; a Fresh Chapter in the History
of Post-Office Reform (1881). Compare Mr. Pearson Hill's tract,
"A Paper on Postage Stamps," in reply to Mr. Chalmers, reprinted from
the "Philatelic Record," of November, 1881." Mr. Hill has therein shown
conclusively the priority of *publication* by Sir Rowland Hill. He has also
given proof of Mr. James Chalmers' express acknowledgment of that
priority. But he has not weakened the evidence of the priority of *invention*
by Mr. Chalmers.

[This admission on the part of Mr. Chalmers, obtained through an
obscuring and consequent misapprehension of the facts, was, of course,
wholly invalid. Even if valid, it will be seen at page 44 that such priority
of publication of an idea "suggested from without" was of no practical
consequence.—P.C.]

" won local distinction in matters of postal
" reform by his strenuous and successful efforts,
" made as early as in the year 1822, for
" the acceleration of the Scottish mails from
" London. Those efforts resulted in a saving of
" forty-eight hours on the double journey, and
" were highly appreciated in Scotland. There is
" evidence that from 1822 onwards his attention
" was much directed towards postal questions,
" and that he held correspondence with the postal
" reformers of his day both in and out of Parlia-
" ment. It is also plain that he was more intent
" upon aiding public improvements than upon
" winning credit for them. He made adhesive
" stamps in 1834, and showed them to his neigh-
" bours, but took no step for publicly recommend-
" ing their adoption by the Post Office until long
" after such a recommendation had been published
" —although very hesitatingly—by the author
" of the now famous pamphlet entitled ' Post
" Office Reform.'*   Mr. Hill brought the adhesive
" stamp under the notice of the Commissioners
" of Post Office Inquiry on the 13th February,
" 1837. Mr. Chalmers made no *public* mention
" of his stamp of 1834 until December, 1837." †

* " Ninth Report of Commissioners of Post-Office Inquiry, 1837," pp. 32,
33, reprinted in Sir R. Hill's " History of Penny Postage " (" Life," &c.,
ii. 270).

† [That Mr. Chalmers had not made an earlier offer of his stamp
officially is accounted for by the proposals of 1834 with respect to a
penny postage on newspapers, in place of an impressed stamp of fourpence
on the sheet, having come to nothing.—P. C.]

" Only a fortnight before his examination by
" the above-named Commissioners Mr. Hill, in
" his letter to the late Lord Monteagle (then Mr.
" Spring Rice, and Chancellor of the Exchequer),
" seems to have had no thought of the *adhesive*
" stamp.   He recommends to the Treasury ' that
" ' stamped covers and sheets of paper be supplied
" ' to the public from the Stamp Office or Post
" ' Office   .   .   .   and sold at such a price as to
" ' include the postage . . . . .   Covers at
" ' various prices would be required for packets of
" ' various weights.   Each should have the weight
" ' it is entitled to carry legibly printed with the
" ' stamp . . . .   Should experience warrant
" ' the Government in making the use of stamped
" ' covers universal,* most important advantages
" ' would be secured.   The Post Office would be
" ' relieved altogether from the collection of the
" ' revenue.'†

   " Then, upon suggestion, it would seem, of
" some possible difficulty that might arise from
" the occasional bringing to a post-office by per-
" sons unable to write, of unstamped letters, he
" added : ' Perhaps this difficulty might be ob-
" ' viated by using a bit of paper just large enough
" ' to bear the stamp, and covered at the back
" ' with a glutinous wash.'   It is a quite fair in-
" ference that this alternative had been sug-

* *I.e.*, by prohibiting the prepayment of letters in money.
† "Ninth Report," as above.

" gested from without.* In reviewing the sub-
" ject, long afterwards, in his 'History of
" ' Penny Postage,' Sir R. Hill says : ' The Post-
" ' Office opinions as to the use of stamps for . .
" ' prepayment were on the whole favourable.' †
" In a paper of 1839, entitled ' On the Collection
" ' of Postage by means of Stamps,' the author
" continued to look upon ' stamped covers or
" ' envelopes as the means which the public would
" ' most commonly employ ; still believing that
" ' the adhesive stamp would be reserved for
" ' exceptional cases.'

    " Mulready's well-remembered allegorical cover
" came into use on 1st May, 1840, together with
" the first form of the stamped letter-paper, and
" the adhesive labels. They all met at first, but
" only for a few days, with a large sale. That of
" the first day yielded £2,500. Soon afterwards
" the public rejection of the ' Mulready envelope,'
" writes Rowland Hill, ' was so complete as to
" ' necessitate the destruction of nearly all the
" ' vast number prepared for issue.' Whilst, on

* Moreover, what Sir Rowland Hill does *not* tell in his " History," is
that the compulsion to use a stamp in all cases was, in his *original*
evidence in this Ninth Report, at once *withdrawn*, the permission to pay
the penny in cash being restored, so that the person " unable to write "
was at once relieved of all " difficulty," and no bit of gummed paper
required even in the exceptional case supposed. (See my former pamphlet,
page 56.) Keeping this fact in view, there is thus only a passing " allusion " here in February, 1837, to the adhesive stamp, and nothing more,
not even a partial proposal to use it. This clause restoring the permission
to pay the penny in place of using any stamp, is taken no notice of by Sir
Rowland Hill " in reviewing the subject long afterwards."—P.C.]

† " History of Penny Postage," as above.   ‡ *Ibid.*

" the other hand, the presses of the Stamp Office
" were producing more than half a million of
" [adhesive] labels, by working both night and
" day, they yet failed to meet the demand.* It
" was only after many weeks, and after the intro-
" duction of a series of mechanical improvements
" and new processes, due to the skill and ingenuity
" in part of Mr. Edwin Hill of the Stamp Office,
" in part of Mr. Perkins, an engraver, that the
" demand could be effectually answered."

The above emphatic decision on the part of
eminent men whom I have never seen in favour
of James Chalmers as having been the inventor of
the adhesive postage stamp, will give much satisfaction in those numerous quarters from which I
have already met with countenance and support.
After a full consideration of the respective statements put forward by myself and by Mr. Pearson
Hill on the subject, James Chalmers at length
obtains a recognition of which he has, as a rule,
been only too long deprived. And that the same
man who invented this stamp also first proposed
its adoption has been already too clearly shown
to require repetition here. Surely Sir Rowland
Hill's " paper of 1839," mentioned in this article,
was a trifle behindhand, when I have just proved
from Sir Henry Cole's papers that Mr. Chalmers
had already laid his plan before Mr. Hill himself
in February, 1838. Did Mr. Hill tell us *that* in

* Hill, *et supra*, p. 398.

his paper of 1839 ? No. Did he tell us that he drew up this paper of 1839 under a pressing demand for the adhesive stamp from all quarters ? No. *Was it fair of Sir Rowland Hill to allow the readers of his " History of Penny Postage," or of his paper of* 1839, *to conclude that this proposal on his part of* 1839 *was put forward of his own initiation, and this with Mr. Chalmers' plan and statement of February,* 1838, *already in his possession ?* A plan which, in his reply to Mr. Chalmers of 3rd March following, Mr. Hill had pooh-poohed ! Moreover, in referring to this " paper of 1839 " in his " History of Penny Postage," vol. 1, page 346, Sir Rowland Hill takes special credit to himself for having therein recommended that the adhesive stamps " should be printed on sheets," putting same forward as a further idea of his own, and wholly ignoring the fact of such having been a special feature, " for sale in sheets or singly," in that plan of Mr. Chalmers *which lay before him.* (See *ante,* page 24.) It is unfortunate that the writer of this article was not at the time of writing in possession of the whole facts of the case, when doubtless Mr. Hill's " paper of 1839 " would have been characterised as it deserved. Sir Rowland Hill's mode of obtaining credit for " inventions " or proposals of other men will now be better understood.

If Mr. Hill alluded to this adhesive stamp (the admitted invention of Mr. Chalmers in 1834) in

February, 1837, while Mr. Chalmers urged its adoption officially only in December, this, it will be seen, arose from Mr. Hill having been privileged to give evidence on postal affairs before the Commissioners of Inquiry. The proposal of 1834 with respect to newspapers came to nothing; consequently there was no opening *then* for Mr. Chalmers to send in his invention *officially*. In sending in his plan to the Select Committee of the House of Commons in December, 1837, Mr. Chalmers was still a year and a half before the Penny Postage Bill was even introduced into Parliament. Mr. Hill did not adopt same until he issued his " paper of 1839." Mr. Hill's allusion to this stamp in February, 1837, this "publishing " of the idea " very hesitatingly," had no practical effect whatever on the cause in hand; such only shows that Mr. Hill had heard of the invention of 1834, without seeing its value or proposing to adopt it. Moreover, Mr. Chalmers was publishing his own invention, while Mr. Hill was only publishing an acquired idea, " suggested " from without." It is to the man who not only invented the adhesive postage stamp, but who further first urged the adoption of same in its entirety for the purpose of carrying out the Penny Postage scheme, that the merit of this plan and of its results are due and will be ascribed.

But if I was to stop here I should be told now, as I have been told before on obtaining important recognitions, that the present decision in my favour was again got upon mere *ex-parte* statements — that had Mr. Pearson Hill only been given the opportunity, a very different aspect would have been put upon the matter. No choice, consequently, is left me but to show that it is to Mr. Pearson Hill himself I am indebted for the introduction which has led to my success, and without which introduction, now reproduced, I should have remained in entire ignorance as to any forthcoming article upon postal affairs, or have been most courteously afforded an opportunity of stating my case :—

[Copy.]
" ENCYCLOPÆDIA BRITANNICA."
" 50, BELSIZE PARK,
" LONDON, N.W.,
" 15*th March*, 1883.
" GENTLEMEN,

" As you are now issuing a new edition of " your ' Encyclopædia Britannica,' and as for " years past a Mr. Patrick Chalmers has per- " sistently been making false and groundless " charges against my father, the late Sir Rowland " Hill, I think it well to send you the enclosed " printed documents for your information, as it is " by no means improbable that he may strive to " get you to insert some untrue statement when " you deal with the question of the Post Office " and Postal Reform.

" I need hardly say that I shall be happy at
" any time to submit to you the original documents
" which are in my possession, which disprove the
" claims put forward in behalf of Mr. James
" Chalmers of Dundee, if you would desire to see
" them.

" Your statistical information about the Post
" Office, as given in my copy of the Encyclopædia
" (the eighth edition) is of course now much
" behindhand. I dare say you have already on
" your staff of contributors some gentleman well
" able to supply you with fresh information ; but
" should you be in want of any such help, I feel
" sure that my cousin, Mr. Lewin Hill, head of
" the statistical branch of the Secretary's office,
" General Post Office, London, would gladly
" undertake the work if you desired it.

" I am, Gentlemen,

" Your obedient servant,

" (Signed) PEARSON HILL.

" Messrs. A. & C. Black,
    " Edinburgh."

It is thus manifest that, in having obtained this
conclusive recognition, I have taken no undue
advantage of Mr. Pearson Hill, while it will also
be manifest that Mr. Pearson Hill's statements
have found acceptance in other quarters only
because I have not been afforded an equally im-

partial hearing as in the present case. His printed documents, his statements, with all the advantage of being sole possessor of the correspondence betwixt his late father and mine, have been put forward, and yet the decision is against him.

Again, as respects the penny postage scheme itself, the proofs are conclusive that *originality of conception* formed no element whatever in any one of the proposals of Sir Rowland Hill, preceded and heralded as the penny postage reform had been by the labours of a whole band of pioneers. Special reference may be made to the statements of the Rev. Samuel Roberts, whose biography as the pioneer of uniform penny postal reform is given in the *Times* of 30th September last. The "Rowland Hill Memorial Fund" Committee have themselves admitted, after what has been laid before them, their sense of this non-originality by the change made in the inscription upon the City statue of Sir Rowland Hill, thereby confirming the accuracy of my statements. Moreover, a Treasury Minute of 11th March, 1864, distinctly states that uniform penny postage had been urged upon the Government prior to the proposals of Sir Rowland Hill. Thus, independent and conclusive testimony, as distinguished from the mere family tradition with which many writers have hitherto been content, leaves the question of plagiarism beyond dispute. As with

---

the stamp, so with the scheme, the ideas were *acquired, not original.* Here, then, is the justification of my statements. So far from having been " persistently making false and groundless " charges," I have been stating facts and elucidating the truth, and the aspersions of Mr. Pearson Hill are thus scattered to the winds.

For Mr. Pearson Hill, however, every allowance will be made, though his style of controversy will not be admired. That gentleman forgets that my motives and objects are just as legitimate as his own, and should be met in a legitimate way. This leads me to mention that some time ago Mr. Samuel Morley, M.P. (at one period chairman of the " Sir Rowland Hill Memorial Fund " Committee) was good enough to suggest that this controversy should be decided by arbitration, and to which I agreed in principle, subject to due preliminaries, but met with no response. At a later period, in a letter already published, after pointing to my own evidence, I invited Mr. Morley's good offices, seeing that Mr. Pearson Hill declined to reply to or even to open any letter from me, to ascertain from Mr. Hill if he could produce any evidence, or anything beyond mere assumption, to the effect that the adhesive postage stamp was at any period an invention on the part of Sir Rowland Hill, but I was equally unsuccessful in obtaining any reply, there being, in fact, nothing beyond assumption in the matter. Nowhere does Sir Rowland Hill directly profess that this stamp was his invention.

My friends, both in and out of the press, who have been puzzled at the silence of many of the London papers on this subject, will now be in a position to form some conclusion as to the cause of this silence. What has been sent to the Messrs. Black and to the Commissioners of City Sewers, may have been sent to the London papers ; indeed, I have been given to understand has been generally circulated in these quarters, already compromised in their expressed opinions, and so in no way disposed to entertain fresh views.* My opponents, some of them in high position, others themselves connected with the press, are desirous, and naturally so, that public attention should not be drawn to my statements.†
In this way, crushed beneath the weight of a hitherto great name, statements have been disregarded which, when read and investigated as in the case of the " Encyclopædia Britannica," have been found substantiated.

---

* In lately replying to Mr. Pearson Hill in the columns of the *Whitehall Review*, I have put this query, which has not been denied, " Will Mr. Pearson Hill undertake to say that he has not made a communication, written or verbal, similar to the above letter to Messrs. A. & C. Black to every editor in London, if not throughout a wider sphere ? "

† One mode of stifling the subject has been to circulate the impression that I am a person under the hallucination that " his father invented the *Penny Postage scheme*," thus rendering my claim too ludicrous to obtain attention. See, amongst others, the *Times* and *Daily News* of 13th July, 1881.

I ask my supporters and others, therefore, to
read and judge for themselves. Whether the
London papers, hitherto silent, seeing the important recognition my claim has now met with,
and the fresh and conclusive evidence now dis-
closed from the papers of Sir Henry Cole, will also
now read and admit some discussion of this matter
of public interest in their columns, remains to be
seen. In any case, an enduring record of my
father's share in the great postal reform of
1837–40 is secured. A work of the highest
standing, and a reference to which is the first act
of historical writers, has recorded James Chalmers
as having been the originator of that adhesive
postage stamp which saved the reformed scheme.
Moreover, in lands beyond the sea, an interest is
taken in this subject wholly unknown here; in-
dividuals and learned societies collect for their
own information, and hand down for future
perusal, everything published on the great Penny
Postage reform, and in some of these quarters
amazement is expressed at the single-hero-worship
which prevails in this country with respect to a
subject which investigation shows to have been
the offspring of many minds, the result of the
labours of not a few zealous but unassuming men.

The services of Sir Rowland Hill, already cordially recognised in my pamphlets, it would be
superfluous again to dwell upon here. And if,
while cordially pointing out these great services,

it has also fallen to my lot to put a fresh and less
favourable aspect upon their nature and extent
than hitherto understood, to bring to light his
great failing of assuming or allowing to be assumed
as conceptions of his own what were only acquired
ideas, of omitting to notice what it was not con-
venient to notice, let it be remembered that such
has been forced upon me as a necessity solely in
the pursuit of what is now declared to have been
a just claim.   At one period, indeed, I had withdrawn from the whole matter, until recalled to it
by Mr. Pearson Hill himself in a published statement to which I was challenged to reply.   My
replies, under ever - increasing and conclusive
evidence, have now been put forward.   Should
the result not have proved such as the best friends
of Sir Rowland Hill could have desired, upon his
own son, and not upon me, rests the responsibility.
It is enough for me that my father's memory as
the originator and inventor of the adhesive
postage stamp has been successfully vindicated.

VALUE AND IMPORTANCE OF THE ADHESIVE STAMP.

" Why should we be called upon to pass this " Penny Postage Bill," said the opponents of that measure in August, 1839, " when no mortal being " had at that moment the remotest conception of " how it was to be carried into execution ? " Mr. Rowland Hill's plan of the impressed stamp had not satisfied the Committee. This plan, as amended by the Committee, had not satisfied the Government. (See *ante*, page 13.) The paper makers and stationers were in a state of protest and alarm. " This part of the business " must stand over, " said the Government of the day, " How to carry out the scheme will require " much consideration." It was here that James Chalmers, through Mr. Wallace, Chairman of the Committee, stepped in—the adhesive stamp saved the scheme. *That* was the value and importance of his invention and proposal. It satisfied the paper trade; "Let the stationer, not "the Stamp Office," said Mr. Chalmers, " sell the paper, the Post Office " the stamp." He saved the scheme of Mr. Hill to the country by relieving and setting agoing the clogged wheels of penny postage—he supplied the engines to the much admired but immovable craft and sent her speeding smoothly and swiftly upon her beneficent mission.

No wonder Sir Rowland Hill determined that no name but his own should be heard of in connection with the adhesive stamp, for of what use is a scheme, however desirable, if you cannot carry it out in practice ?   This is what he admits on the subject soon after the simultaneous introduction of the Mulready envelope and the adhesive stamp— " The public rejection of the former was so com- " plete as to necessitate the destruction of nearly " all the vast number prepared for issue." On the other hand—" Though the presses of the " Stamp Office were producing more than half a " million of adhesive stamps by working both " night and day, they yet failed to meet the " demand." Up to this day, after over forty years of public service, and notwithstanding the improvements in the production of impressed and embossed stamps, the adhesive stamp remains indispensable to our postal, inland revenue, telegraphic, and parcel-post systems—" Eighteen " hundred millions are issued *yearly* from the office " of the Controller of stamps. These range in value " from a halfpenny to twenty pounds, covering " postage and inland revenue from a halfpenny to " two shillings and sixpence ; postage proper from " five shillings to five pounds ; inland revenue

" proper (such as foreign bills, sea policy stamps,
" &c.) from one penny to ten pounds ; and fees
" (such as judicature, &c), from one penny to twenty
" pounds. The penny stamp takes the first place
" amongst the numbers issued. Of these, as many
" as thirteen hundred millions and a half were de-
" spatched from Somerset House in the course of
" a recent twelvemonth."* Twenty-five millions of
parcels are now annually conveyed by Parcel Post,
a business only practicable through prepayment
by adhesive stamp.

Thus, ever increasing in utility, thus indispensable to the carrying out of all or any of
these great public services, the value of James
Chalmers' invention and proposal—the importance
of this "powerful mechanism of the stamp"—may
be best felt by the consideration that its suspen-
sion, even for a day, would paralyse the entire
commercial and social system of the nation, it
may be said "of the world" for in all other
lands, one after another, has the adhesive stamp
become an institution for similar purposes as in
our own, and in corresponding numbers.

In this sense an eminent writer has lately
stated, " Whoever discovered the adhesive stamp,
" the discovery has socially revolutionised the
" world." " Should my plan be adopted," was
the prophetic saying of Mr. Chalmers when he sent
his plan to London and to Mr. Hill himself, long

* " Chambers' Journal," March, 1885.

before the Penny Postage Bill was even introduced into Parliament, " should my adhesive
" stamp be adopted, the demand for these will in
" time become so vast, that I am only puzzled to
" think where premises can be found to get them
" up." Surely the man who rescued the Legislature from such a complication as has been
described, surely the originator of this indispensable and ubiquitous adhesive stamp has done
the State some service.

CONCLUSION.

Objections have been raised, both in and out of the press, to the effect that my claim comes " too " late in the day." Such objection will, I believe, be found effectually met in my preface and former pamphlets, to the satisfaction of any impartial mind favouring me with a perusal.

With those who decline to read my statements, amongst whom may be named several writers of biography wrapt up in a blind worship of pre-conceived ideas, nothing, of course, can be done.

Others say, " Get an official recognition of your " claim from the Post Office, then we will re- " cognise you." This, again, is taking matters in the reverse order ; if the Post Office is ever to recognise me, the pressure must come from outside, as the Post Office, under its late chief, Mr. Shaw Lefevre, simply declines to read or cause to be read for its imformation anything I may lay before it, as " not being deemed necessary." As I have nothing to ask from that quarter, having now gained a recognition promising to be sufficient for my purpose, I have no present intention of again troubling the Post Office on the subject. The feeling of *esprit de corps*, if nothing else, will probably render the Post Office the very last body to admit that any mistake by the late Sir Rowland Hill has been made.

But it may be said, " Did not the Post Office give " Palmer, the organiser of the mail-coach system, " in addition to his pay of £3,000 a year, £50,000?" And was not James Chalmers the successor in that line, sixty years ago, of Palmer? Yes— but then Mr. Palmer was a man of business, and had made his bargain with the Post Office *before* he took the mail-coach organisation in hand to be .paid according to results; while, after all, the £50,000 was only a compromise, obtained, moreover, only after the repeated inter- ference of Parliament. James Chalmers, recog- nised by the leading Scottish press of the period, and by his townsmen, never dreamt of asking a pecuniary reward. Again, was not the Post Office in 1852 most liberal with Archer, the in- ventor of the perforating machine—did they not give him £4,000 for the use of it? Yes—but then Mr. Archer had taken out a patent for his inven- tion, and refused to sell the use of it for less, and it was not until after a fruitless negotiation of five years, ending in a Parliamentary Committee taking up the subject and insisting upon Mr. Archer being paid his moderate demand, that the Post Office and the Treasury gave in, and but for this Parliamentary pressure we might yet be cutting off our stamps with a pair of scissors to this day.

In the same way, then, it has been asked, would not an infinitesimal royalty on the increasing millions of adhesive stamps have long ago placed that originator, him and his, amongst the wealthy of the land? Yes—but such was not the spirit in which James Chalmers trafficked and trifled with the public interests. What are his last words to Sir Rowland Hill on the subject? "The only " satisfaction I have had in this, as well as in " former suggestions, all original to me, is that " these have been adopted, and have and are " likely to prove beneficial to the public." This was the spirit in which the originator of the adhesive stamp ever tendered his services, public or private—the satisfaction of finding them useful and accepted. In the continued and ever-increasing utility of his stamp may be seen that silent yet irresistible tribute of the nation to its originator which James Chalmers would most have prized— only, let the hand which gave it be rightly known and recognised. For a time powerful influences to silence may prevail and popular delusion continue to hold its sway. But at some future day, if not now—in other lands if not in this—will the name of James Chalmers be yet recognised in connection with our constant friend and companion, the adhesive stamp, and the great boon of Penny Postage reform.

APPENDIX.

DUNDEE.

So satisfied were the Dundee merchants of a past age as to the originality and value of Mr. Chalmers' invention and happy suggestion that, on the 1st January, 1846, a public Testimonial was presented to him in the Town Hall of Dundee in recognition of same and of other postal services. This Testimonial consisted of a silver jug and salver and a purse of 50 sovereigns. Just before this period, Mr. Rowland Hill had been presented by the merchants of the City of London with a cheque for over £13,000, in recognition of what now turns out to have been merely a borrowed scheme, and which scheme was only saved from untimely collapse by the adoption of Mr. Chalmers' plan of the adhesive stamp.

In the present generation, again, the Town Council of Dundee have performed a graceful act to the memory of a deserving townsman, by having passed at a meeting held on the 3rd March, 1883, the following resolution :—

"That, having had under consideration the Pamphlet "lately published on the subject of the Adhesive Stamp, the "Council are of opinion that it has been conclusively shown "that the late James Chalmers, bookseller, Dundee, was the "originator of this indispensable feature in the success of "the reformed Penny Postage Scheme, and that such be "entered upon the minutes."

The above resolution of the Town Council is now, it will be seen, fully confirmed by the able and learned writers of the "Encyclopædia Britannica," after an impartial investigation of the subject—a confirmation having all the greater weight as reversing, upon evidence which could not be resisted, previously recorded impressions.

Dundee is now a large and wealthy community, returning two members to Parliament; few centres of business have benefited more conspicuously from the legislation of the past forty years, including as the foundation of all mercantile intercourse that great postal reform which James Chalmers saved from failure and made practicable. Two generations have already recognised and given every credit to the services of their townsman—what further notice Dundee may yet take of this matter of national and historical interest originated in the locality, the "value and importance" of which has elsewhere been inadequately described, remains to be seen.

OPINIONS FROM THE PRESS.

HAVING already published most of these in detail, to save space and repetition it will be sufficient here to give a list or little more, of the numerous Journals which have given me more or less support.

Those to which I am more particularly indebted are:—
In Scotland—

The "Dundee Advertiser," a consistent support during a past lengthened period, including powerful leading articles and notices.

The "Montrose Standard," several cordial and able articles of the highest value, while the same is to be gratefully noticed of the other Forfarshire papers,

The "Brechin Advertiser," the "Forfar Herald," the "Arbroath Guide," the "Montrose Review."

The "North British Daily Mail," of Glasgow, in a leading article headed "A Neglected Inventor," after stating the case, goes on to say: "It is not creditable to the generosity of "the Government of this country that an important invention

" of this kind, which has conferred such a great boon upon the
" public, should have remained so long unacknowledged and
" unrewarded." This article has been extensively reproduced.

The " Glasgow News " and the " Christian Leader," of
Glasgow, cordial articles.

The " Paisley Herald," the same on several occasions.

The " Aberdeen Free Press," a warm and able support.

The " Blairgowrie Advertiser " has taken much interest
and pains to support me ; also the " Perthshire Constitutional,"
the " Fifeshire Journal," the " North British Advertiser," to
all of which my best thanks are due.

In the Metropolis and neighbourhood, considering how
short a period has elapsed since the opinion has been almost
unanimously expressed that the reformed Penny Postage
scheme was the " sole and undisputed invention of Sir Rowland
" Hill," to whom has also been erroneously attributed the
invention and proposal as well as the ultimate adoption of the
adhesive stamp, fair progress has already been made in
obtaining a recognition of Mr. Chalmers' services. That
greater progress has not been made may be attributed to the
powerful influences which have been at work to stifle the
whole subject, including an attempt on the part of
Mr. Pearson Hill to stop the publication of pamphlets.

In the " Illustrated London News " Mr. G. A. Sala
writes : " It seems tolerably clear that Sir Rowland Hill was
" not the inventor, in the strict sense of the term, either of
" the Penny Postage or of the Adhesive Postage Stamp. . .
" Anent the invention of the Adhesive Stamp, a pamphlet
" has recently been published, but I have not yet had time
" to read it. . . . Whoever discovered the Adhesive
" Stamp, the discovery has socially revolutionised the world.'
According to this high authority, the Adhesive Stamp was
thus at least *not* the invention of Sir Rowland Hill.

The " Whitehall Review " has given me consistent and
most valuable support ; also the " Metropolitan," the " People,"
the " Home and Colonial Mail." The " Machinery Market,"
of London and Darlington, a practical monthly journal of
high position, while retaining all its former admiration for

Sir Rowland Hill's services, decides, in a long and able article, in favour of James Chalmers as respects the stamp. The "Inventors' Record," in an article on "Disputed Inventions," supports the same view. The pretensions brought forward on the part of Sir Rowland Hill are declared to be wholly groundless, and the invention accorded to James Chalmers.

The "Croydon Review," a monthly, in a series of able articles, has informed its readers candidly with respect to the untenable pretensions of Sir Rowland Hill, both as respects the scheme and the stamp, cordially ascribing the latter to James Chalmers.

The "Surrey Independent" has ably supported me in several leading articles. As far as conception went, "Sir "Rowland Hill displayed a remarkable facility for picking "other people's brains,"

To the "Surrey Comet" and "Wimbledon Courier" my best thanks are due for cordial notices and recognition; as also to the "West Middlesex Advertiser," the "South "Hampstead Advertiser," the "North Middlesex Advertiser," the "Christian Union," the "Hornsey and Finsbury Park "Journal," the "American Bookseller," the "Acton and "Chiswick Gazette," "Figaro," "Vanity Fair," the "Kensington News," "Life," and others.

From the Provincial Press, much valuable support has been given me :—

The "Oldham Chronicle" and "Rastrick Gazette" have written often and ably on the subject, supported by such papers as the "Bradford Observer," the "Western Daily "Press," of Bristol, the "Bristol Gazette," the "Norwich "Argus," the "Brighton Herald," the "Brighton Argus," the "Dover and County Chronicle," the "Colchester "Chronicle," the "Stratford and South Essex Advertiser," the "Essex Standard," the "Bradford Times," the "Burnley "Express," the "Barnsley Times," the "Wigan Observer," the "Stockport Advertiser," the "Yorkshire Gazette," the "Westmoreland Gazette," the "Wakefield and West Riding "Herald," the "Frome Times;" the "Man of Ross," the

" Totnes Times," the " Banner of Wales," the " West
" Bromwich Free Press," the " Swinton and Pendlebury
" Times," the " Accrington Gazette," the " Birkenhead
" News," the " Brighton Standard," the " Hastings Observer,"
the " Newcastle Courant," the " Preston Chronicle," the
" Monmouthshire Beacon," the " Lydney Observer," the
" West of England Observer," the " Cardiff Free Press,' the
" Monmouthshire Chronicle," the " Eskdale and Liddlesdale
" Advertiser," the " Irvine Express," the " Surrey Advertiser,"
the " Printers' Register," the " Newcastle Examiner," the
" Malvern News," and others, with articles sympathetically
copied into the " Brighton Guardian," the " Aberdeen
" Journal," the " Dundee Courier," The " Edinburgh
" Courant," the " Liverpool Albion," the " Building and
" Engineering Times " of London," &c.

The late Sir Thomas Nelson, Solicitor to the Corporation
of the City of London, writes :—

" HAMPTON WICK,
" 6th February, 1883.
" SIR,

" I have read the pamphlet you sent me. Your
" statements are very interesting. It is nothing uncommon
" for the man to whom the idea first occurs to have it
" developed by others, who get the credit of it.

" Yours truly,
" (Signed)   T. J. NELSON.
" PATRICK CHALMERS, Esq.
" Wimbledon."

If plagiarism is not uncommon it is none the less unfair to
the original inventor, nor the less to be deprecated, more
especially where the result has been to obtain unmerited
" credit " heaped upon the wrong man at the expense of the
man to whom " the idea first occurred," and who further, as
is now more fully proved since Sir Thomas Nelson wrote, also
first urged its " development " to the very man who
ultimately took all the " credit " to himself. To plagiarism
such as this a stronger term is applicable.

Sir Bartle Frere writes :—

" WRESSIL LODGE, WIMBLEDON,

21*st April*, 1883.

" SIR,

" I have received your letter of the 20th, and thank " you for its enclosures on the subject of the invention of the " adhesive postage stamp.

" I have long believed that Mr. James Chalmers was the " inventor of that important part of our present postal system, " but I regret that I cannot suggest to you any means of " giving further publicity to your father's claims to the merit " of that most useful invention.

" I remain, SIR,

" Yours truly,

" (Signed) H. B. E. FRERE.

" P. CHALMERS, Esq."

Sir Bartle Frere introduced the adhesive postage stamp into Scinde during his administration of that province, having obtained his knowledge and belief as to James Chalmers having been the originator of same from independent sources thirty years before my own investigation of the subject.

In some quarters this matter is ignored on the ground that the subject of this pamphlet is not of sufficient import-ance or too late to call for notice. To such I reply—" Then let the issue of the adhesive stamp (see page 52) be discon-tinued." Should it be found that such cannot be done without serious detriment to the public service, then surely to continue to use a man's indispensable invention and proposal without so much as a word of recognition, will, if adhered to, prove a course of proceeding hard indeed to justify, as well as some-thing wholly foreign to the antecedents of British journalism.

EFFINGHAM WILSON, Printer, Royal Exchange, E.C.

www.ingramcontent.com/pod-product-compliance
Lightning Source LLC
Chambersburg PA
CBHW021630270326
41931CB00008B/949